MAKE IT!

Circuitry and Electronics

Anastasia Suen

Rourke
Educational Media

rourkeeducationalmedia.com

SUPPLIES TO COMPLETE ALL PROJECTS:

- alligator clip wire units
- batteries (AA, button cell, 9 volt)
- battery pack with wire leads
- box with lid (shoe box, gift box)
- chalk
- clear tape
- colored tissue paper
- conductive thread
- copper nails
- copper tape
- galvanized nails
- glue or glue stick
- knit gloves
- LED lights
- low voltage LED clock

- modeling clay
- needle
- newspaper or paper towels to cover the work area
- paper
- paper clip (large)
- pencil
- plastic placemat or wax paper to cover your work area
- Play-Doh
- potatoes
- scissors

Table of Contents

Circuits and Electronics

Yes, you can make your own *electronic* devices!

Turn on a light with pencil lead. Run a clock with two potatoes. Experiment with Play-Doh power. Make cell phone gloves. Transform a shoe box into a colored light for your room. Who knew circuits could be so much fun?

Paper Circuit

YOU WILL NEED:

- pencil
- sheet of paper
- LED light
- tape
- 9-volt battery

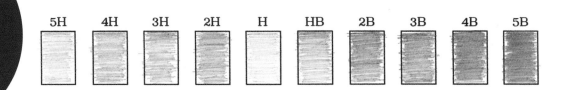

Tip:
Pencil lead is made of graphite. If the graphite rubbed on the paper is thick enough, the light will turn on. For the best results, use an art pencil.

5H	4H	3H	2H	H	HB	2B	3B	4B	5B

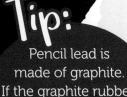

TURN ON A LIGHT WITH PAPER AND A PENCIL!

Here's How:

1. Draw two thick lines that do not touch.

2. Make a plus sign at both ends of one line.

3. Make a minus sign at both ends of the other line.

Make the ends of the two lines approximately 3/8 inch (10 millimeters) apart so each end will touch a terminal in the battery.

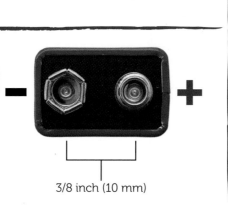

3/8 inch (10 mm)

Bend the LED wires. Bend one wire to the left and the other wire to the right.

 Tape the longer wire to the line with the plus sign.

 Tape the shorter wire to the line with the minus sign.

Tip:

The longer LED wire is the positive wire. The shorter one is the negative wire.

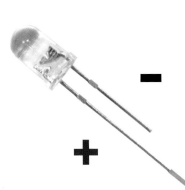

−

+

 Hold the battery on the other side of each line.

8. Touch the plus line with the plus terminal of the battery.

 Touch the minus line with the minus terminal.

Tip:
An LED light glows brightest when it is close to the battery. Experiment with different line lengths and see how long the line can be.

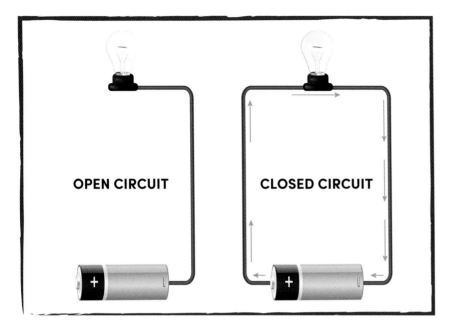

OPEN CIRCUIT

CLOSED CIRCUIT

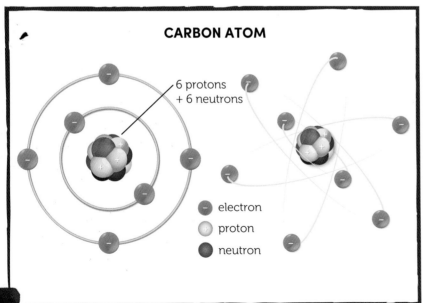

CARBON ATOM

6 protons
+ 6 neutrons

electron
proton
neutron

Why Does It Work?

The carbon in the graphite acts as a conductor. It allows **electricity** to flow through it. When the battery touches both graphite lines, electricity can flow in a **circuit**. It moves from the battery to the light and back to the battery.

The flow of electricity starts on the minus side of the battery. This is because electricity is created by the electrons in **atoms**. The tiny electrons in atoms have negative charges. Everything in the universe is made from atoms, even you!

Potato Clock

- newspaper or paper towels to cover the work area

- 2 potatoes

- 2 galvanized nails

- 2 copper nails

- 3 alligator clip wire units (wire with alligator clips on each end)

- low voltage LED clock

Trip:

Copper nails are used for weather strips and roof flashing.

POWER A CLOCK WITH POTATOES!

Here's How:

1. Place a galvanized (zinc) nail in each potato.

2. Place a copper nail in each potato.

Tip:

Nails are covered with zinc when they are galvanized. Place the galvanized (zinc) nails on the left and the copper nails on the right. Point them in opposite directions.

zinc nail

copper nail

zinc nail

copper nail

3. Open the back of the clock.

 4. Remove the battery.

5. Clip one alligator clip to the positive terminal.

6. Pull the wire toward the first potato.

7. Clip the other side of the wire to a copper nail.

Tip:
Look for the plus sign + inside the battery compartment. It is written in the plastic at the bottom. The minus sign – is on the opposite side.

8. Clip the second wire to the negative terminal.

 9. Pull the second wire toward the second potato.

 10. Connect the second wire to the zinc-covered nail.

 11. Use the third alligator clip to connect the two potatoes.

 12. Place one clip on the zinc-covered nail.

 13. Clip the other side to the copper nail.

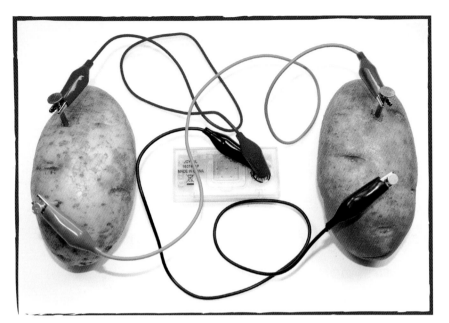

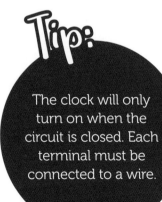

Tip:

The clock will only turn on when the circuit is closed. Each terminal must be connected to a wire.

Why Does It Work?

To make a food battery you need three things: a positive electrode, a negative electrode, and an **electrolyte**. The copper nails are positive **electrodes**. The zinc-coated nails are negative electrodes. The potatoes provide the electrolytes.

Experiment with other foods and see if they can turn on the clock. You may need more than two food batteries to make it work. Connect a wire from each copper nail to a zinc-covered nail in the fruit next to it. Then connect the wires on each end to the clock.

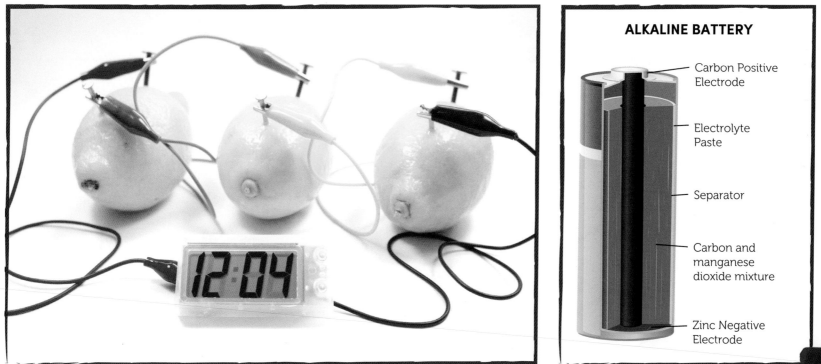

ALKALINE BATTERY

Carbon Positive Electrode

Electrolyte Paste

Separator

Carbon and manganese dioxide mixture

Zinc Negative Electrode

Play-Doh Butterfly Lights

YOU WILL NEED:

- plastic placemat or wax paper to cover your work area

- Play-Doh

- modeling clay

- battery pack with wire leads

- 4 AA batteries for the battery pack

- 2-4 LED lights

LIGHT UP A PLAY-DOH BUTTERFLY!

Here's How:

 1. Roll a log of modeling clay for the body.

2. Make butterfly wings with colored Play-Doh.

3. Place the wings on each side of the body.

Tip: Use different colors for the Play-Doh and the modeling clay.

Play-Doh

modeling clay

4. Pull the LED wires into a wide V.

 5. Press one LED wire in the Play-Doh on the left side.

 6. Press the other LED wire in the Play-Doh on the right.

 7. Repeat for each LED light.

 8. Put the AA batteries in the battery pack.

 9. Poke one wire in the bottom of each wing.

Tip:

You can use the LED lights near the top as antennas. Or you can place the wires on each side of the body to light up the middle.

Why Does It Work?

The salt in the Play-Doh conducts electricity. Electricity flows from the battery pack through the Play-Doh to the LED lights. The circuit is complete.

The modeling clay in the middle is an insulator. It does not conduct electricity. This makes the electricity flow to the LED lights.

Remember the paper circuit? A space between the two conductors also allows the electricity to flow out on one path and flow back on another. Without an insulator or an air gap the LED lights will not turn on. Try it yourself with two rolls of Play-Doh.

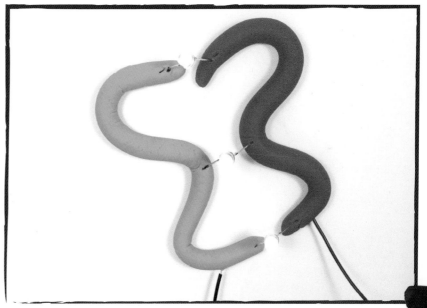

- knit gloves
- chalk
- needle
- conductive thread
- scissors

Touchscreen Gloves

TURN KNIT GLOVES INTO TOUCHSCREEN GLOVES!

Here's How:

 Put on a glove.

 Make a chalk mark where your fingers touch.

 Thread the needle. Tie a knot.

 Sew vertical stitches over the chalk. Cover all of the chalk.

Tip: You can sew conductive thread on all five fingertips or just the thumbs and index fingers.

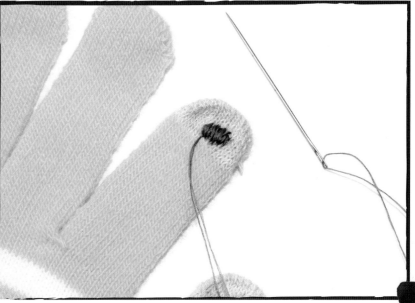

5. Sew a new layer. Sew horizontal stitches over the vertical stitches.

 6. Press the needle inside the glove.

 7. Carefully turn the glove inside out.

 8. Cut the thread. Tie a knot.

 9. Repeat the steps for the next finger.

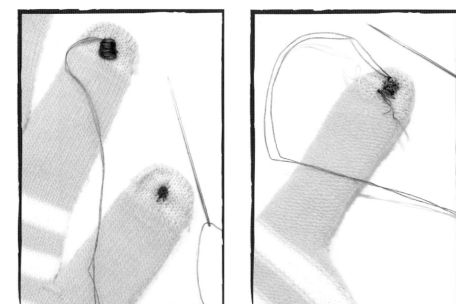

Tip: Add a decorative touch with fabric paint. Paint an outline on each fingertip. Then sew two layers of conductive thread inside the painted outline.

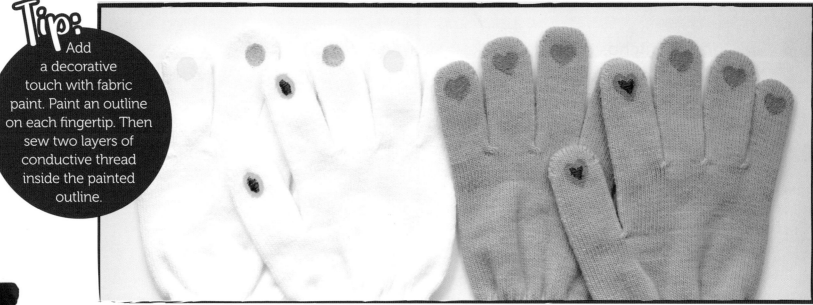

Why Does It Work?

Some phones need the electricity in your finger to complete the circuit. So when you wear gloves, the phone doesn't do anything when you touch it. The gloves insulate your fingers from the cold. They also insulate the electricity in your body.

You can take your gloves off to touch the screen. That makes the phone work, but it doesn't keep your fingers warm.

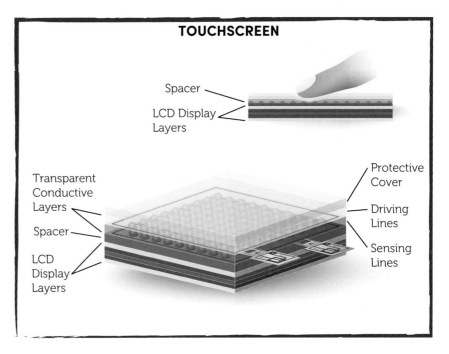

TOUCHSCREEN

Spacer

LCD Display Layers

Transparent Conductive Layers

Spacer

LCD Display Layers

Protective Cover

Driving Lines

Sensing Lines

Sewing conductive thread on the inside and the outside of the gloves does three things:
1. Your fingers stay warm inside the gloves.
2. Your fingers touch the conductive thread inside the gloves.
3. The thread on the inside conducts the electricity from your fingers to the threads on the outside of the gloves. When the electricity from your fingers flows through the conductive thread to the touchscreen, the circuit is complete.

Light Box

- box with lid (shoe box, gift box)
- colored tissue paper
- pencil
- scissors
- glue or glue stick
- paper
- copper tape
- button cell battery
- LED light
- clear tape
- large paper clip

24

MAKE A COLORFUL LIGHT BOX!

Here's How:

 1. Trace the box lid on a sheet of colored tissue paper. Cut out the tissue.

2. Poke a hole in the center of the box lid. Cut the hole into a simple shape.

3. Turn the box lid upside down. Place colored tissue paper over the hole. Glue the tissue inside the lid.

Tip:

Don't cut the shape in the box lid too close to the edge. Leave room along the edges for the glue.

4. Trace the bottom of the box on a sheet of paper. Cut the paper.

5. Put the battery in the upper left corner of the paper. Trace it. Mark the circle with a plus sign.

6. Move the battery right. Trace another circle. Mark the circle with a minus sign.

7. Draw an X in the middle of the paper. That is where the light will go.

8. Now draw a line from the center of each battery circle. Make a square that reaches the X.

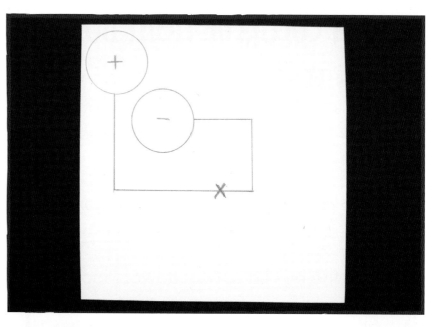

Tip:

When the corner is folded down, the top circle should rest on the lower circle. If it doesn't, erase the lower circle and trace a new one.

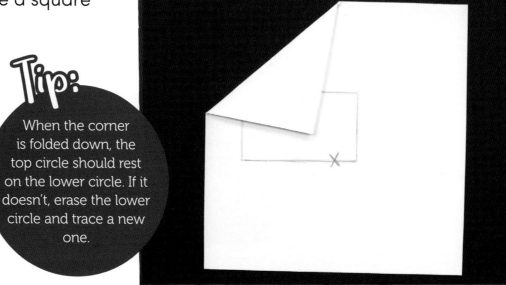

9. Peel the back off the copper tape. Ask an adult to help you.

 10. Press the copper tape on the lines. Fold the tape flat in the corner.

 11. At the end of each line, cut the tape with scissors.

12. Lift the LED wires. Pull one to the left and one to the right.

13. Put the LED light on the X.

14. Cut two small pieces of clear tape.

 15. Use the clear tape to hold the LED wires on the copper tape.

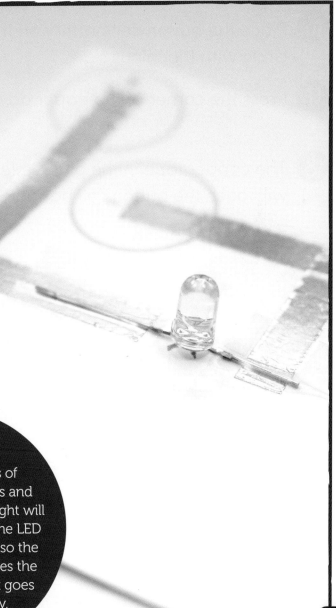

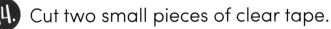

Tip:

Leave a space between the ends of the copper tape lines and the X where the LED light will go. When you place the LED light on the X, turn it so the short LED wire touches the copper tape line that goes under the battery.

16. Place the button cell battery on the circle with the minus sign.

 17. Press the corner of the paper down.

 18. The copper tape in the plus circle will touch the button cell battery.

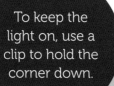

Tip:

To keep the light on, use a clip to hold the corner down.

Why Does It Work?

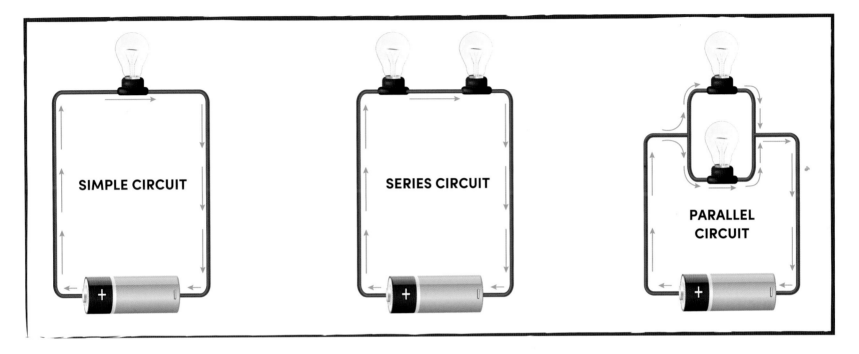

SIMPLE CIRCUIT

SERIES CIRCUIT

PARALLEL CIRCUIT

When you press the corner down, both wires touch the battery. Now the electricity can flow through the wires to the light and back to the battery. The circuit is closed, so the light will turn on.

This light box has a simple circuit, but that is not the only kind of circuit you can build. You can make a light box with a circuit that has more lights and more wires. A series circuit has more than one light on the same wire. Parallel circuits add a new wire for each light. Why not build one of each?

Glossary

atoms (AT-uhms): the smallest part of any item in the universe

circuit (SUR-kit): a complete path that electricity can flow on or through

electricity (i-lek-TRISS-uh-tee): energy created by the movement of protons and electrons

electrodes (i-LEK-trodes): the point where electricity flows in or out of a device, such as a battery

electrolyte (i-LEK-truh-lite): a liquid substance that conducts electricity, such as the juice in a lemon

electronic (e-lik-TRON-ik): a device that is powered by electricity

Index

Show What You Know

1. How do you know that graphite is a conductor?

2. Name the three key elements of a battery.

3. Why was modeling clay used to make the butterfly?

4. Why are touchscreen gloves necessary?

5. Describe a simple circuit.

Websites to Visit

www.explainthatstuff.com/electricity.html

http://sciencewithme.com/learnaboutelectricity/

http://technolojie.com/circuit_sketchbook/

About the Author

Anastasia Suen is the author of more than 250 books for young readers, including *Wired* (A Chicago Public Library Best of the Best Book) about how electricity flows from the power plant to your house. She reads, writes, and edits books in her studio in Northern California.

Meet The Author!
www.meetREMauthors.com

© 2018 Rourke Educational Media

www.rourkeeducationalmedia.com

PHOTO CREDITS: Cover & Pages 4, 5, 6, 7, 8, 9, 11, 12, 13, 14, 15, 16, 17, 18, 19, 20, 21, 22, 24, 25, 26, 27, 28: © creativelytara; Backcover: © tusumaru, © kyoshino; Page 3: © amaking; Page 10 & 15: ©ttsz; Page 10, 23 & 29: © Designua

Edited by: Keli Sipperley
Cover and Interior design by: Tara Raymo • CreativelyTara • www.creativelytara.com

Library of Congress PCN Data

Circuitry and Electronics / Anastasia Suen
(Make It!)
 ISBN 978-1-68342-378-2 (hard cover)
 ISBN 978-1-68342-887-9 (soft cover)
 ISBN 978-1-68342-544-1 (e-Book)
Library of Congress Control Number: 2017934542

Rourke Educational Media
Printed in the United States of America,
North Mankato, Minnesota